P9-DNL-774

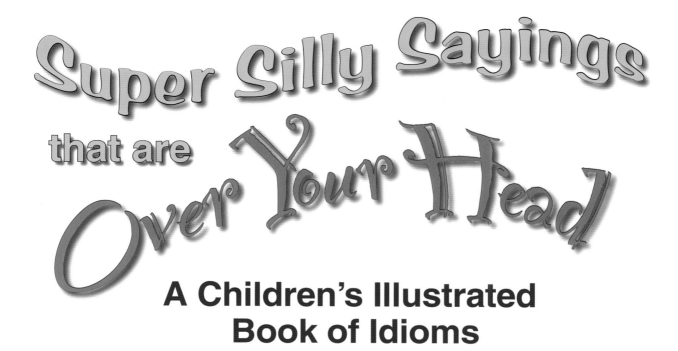

Super Silly Sayings

that are

Over Your Head

A Children's Illustrated
Book of Idioms

by Catherine S. Snodgrass

STARFISH SPECIALTY PRESS

Because it makes a difference to this one

Haverstraw King's Daughters
Public Library
10 W. Ramapo Road
Garnerville, NY 10923

Copyright © 2004 by Catherine S. Snodgrass
Illustrations © Catherine S. Snodgrass

All rights reserved. No part of this book may be reproduced in any form or by any electronic or mechanical means, including photocopying, recording, or any information storage and retrieval system, without written permission from the publisher.

Published in 2004 in the United States of America by Starfish Specialty Press, LLC, PO Box 799, Higganum, CT, 06441-0799

Book layout and design: Patricia Rasch; Cromwell , CT

Questions regarding this book, including ordering information should be addressed to:
Starfish Specialty Press, LLC
P.O. Box 799
Higganum, CT 06441-0799
Phone: 1-877-STARFISH (1-877-782-7347)
E-mail: info@starfishpress.com
Visit us on the Internet at www.starfishpress.com

ISBN: 0-9666529-4-0

Library of Congress Cataloging-in-Publication Data

Snodgrass, Catherine S.
Super silly sayings that are over your head : a children's illustrated book of idioms / by Catherine S. Snodgrass.
p. cm.
Summary: Defines more than forty idioms using an illustration of the literal meaning
next to an illustration of the actual idiomatic meaning and with explanatory text.
ISBN 0-9666529-4-0 (hardcover : alk. paper)
1. English language--Idioms--Juvenile literature. 2. Figures of speech--Juvenile literature.
[1. English language--Idioms. 2. Figures of speech.] I. Title. PE1460 .S59 2004 428--dc22
2003019925

Printed in Hong Kong

10 9 8 7 6 5 4 3 2 1

Catherine S. Snodgrass is an illustrator, painter, and graphic designer. Following a long-term background in the New York City publishing industry, she chose to freelance from her Hudson Valley home in order to spend more time with her children—one of whom has an autism spectrum disorder known as *Asperger syndrome.* Catherine found that after her son's diagnosis some of her responsibilities as a mother shifted, and she took on new roles, such as those of advocate and teacher. Providing an endless supply of unconditional love, understanding, patience, and flexibility—and primed with a great deal of information—she embarked on a new journey as an author with a unique and refreshing perspective. The whimsical and endearing illustrations that grace the pages of *Super Silly Sayings That Are Over Your Head: A Children's Illustrated Book of Idioms* will not only amuse, but also educate children who have difficulty with expressions that say one thing, but actually mean another!

A Note from Catherine S. Snodgrass

I originally decided to put my illustrations to work to educate my son Jesse, since he was having considerable difficulty understanding certain commonly used expressions. Known as idioms, these expressions are typically misinterpreted by individuals in the early stages of language development, and also by those learning a new language. Individuals with autism spectrum disorders (ASD), however, have long-standing difficulty with these expressions, finding them not only confusing, but in some cases, also frightening. For example, how would someone with literal comprehension understand what is meant by the figurative expression, *he stabbed her in the back?* When my son Jesse was eventually diagnosed with Asperger syndrome, a disorder on the autism spectrum, it became obvious to me that his understanding and use of idioms would not simply evolve on their own, without outside assistance.

Among the many challenges that individuals with ASD confront are deficiencies in language, communication, and social interaction. These skills—which most of us take for granted—must be specifically taught to these individuals. Likewise, since individuals with these conditions interpret speech literally, idioms are almost always misunderstood. This makes it even more difficult for people with ASD to navigate in the conventional social world, without someone to serve as an interpreter of these confusing expressions.

In order to help my son effectively process this type of information, I decided to "explain" the meaning of each idiom to him in a way that came naturally to me— through the medium of the visual arts. I first presented my humorous illustrations of each idiom to Jesse in a flash-card format, with accompanying gestures and exaggerated facial expressions to further illuminate their meaning. Jesse's enjoyment was overshadowed only by his actual understanding of the idioms whose meanings he could finally *see*! So began the adventure that led to *Super Silly Sayings That Are Over Your Head: A Children's Illustrated Book of Idioms.* I hope that you will find this book to be suitable for *all* children, most especially those with ASD, foreign language backgrounds, or language learning impairments that make it difficult for them to comprehend figurative language.

How to Use the Fold-out Flap

The flap that follows can be used to cover the written idioms and their explanations to encourage the child to try to figure out the meanings of the idioms from the pictures themselves. Later, it can be used to cover the "answers" to help facilitate recall and independence. The flap may either be kept whole or cut along the dotted lines provided to help minimize distractions and direct the child's attention to the focus of instruction.

This book is dedicated to my son Jesse who
has taught me the true purpose of seeing.

Cut along this line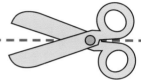

Cut along this line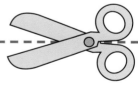

Sometimes people say the strangest things...

I wonder what these super silly sayings really mean.

1

Head

When something is **over your head,** it really means that it is very hard to understand.

When someone says, "**I'm all ears,**" he really means that he is listening very carefully.

If someone tells you to **button your lip,** she really means that you should stop talking.

3

Hands and Feet

If someone asks you to **lend a hand**, she really means that she wants you to **help** her.

When someone says, "I'm **all thumbs**," she really means that she's **clumsy**.

When someone says, "I put my **foot in my mouth**," he really means that he **said something that he shouldn't have said.**

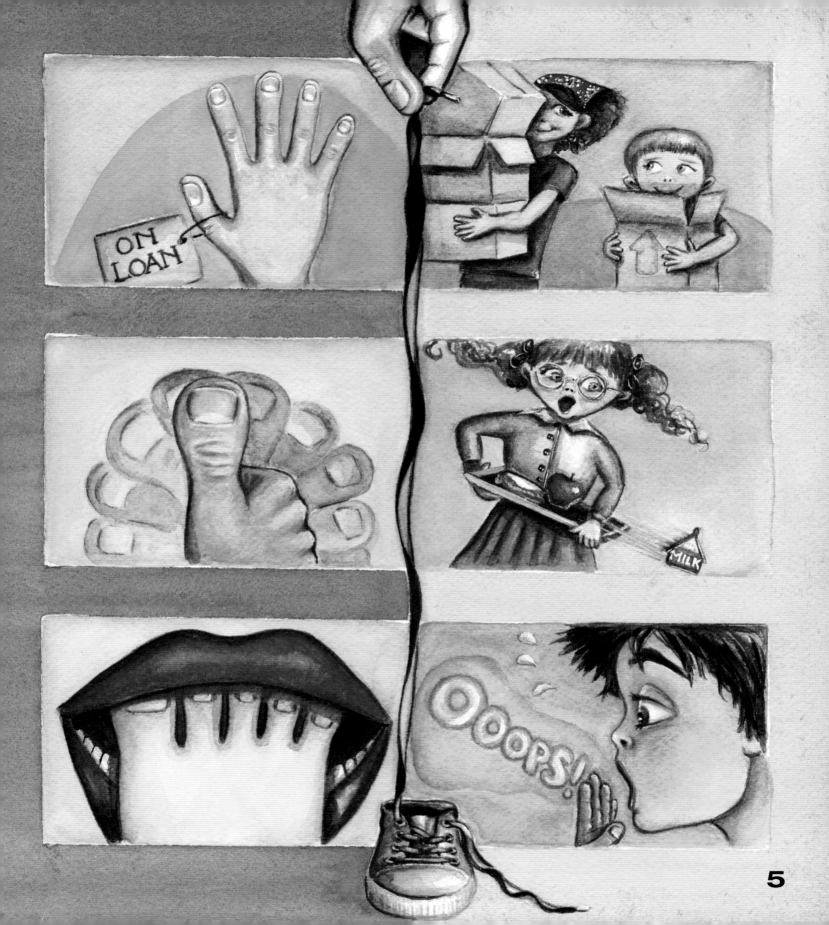

If someone says, "I gave her the **cold shoulder**," she really means that she was **unfriendly** to someone.

When someone says, "I paid **an arm and a leg** for it," he really means that he paid **a high price**.

If someone says, "I have a **broken heart**," she really means that she is **very, very sad**.

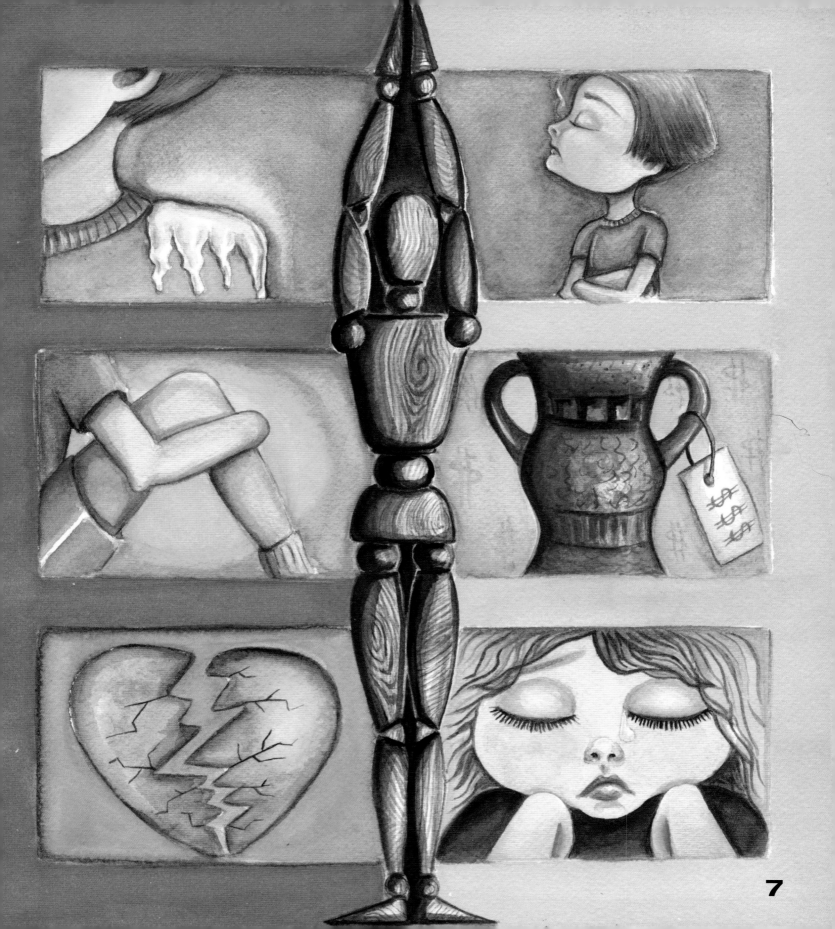

Clothing

If someone says, "You need to **keep your shirt on**," he really means that you need to **stay calm**.

When someone says, "It **knocked my socks off**," she really means that something was **amazing**.

If someone says "I wore my **birthday suit** in the bathtub," he really means that he was **not wearing clothes**.

8

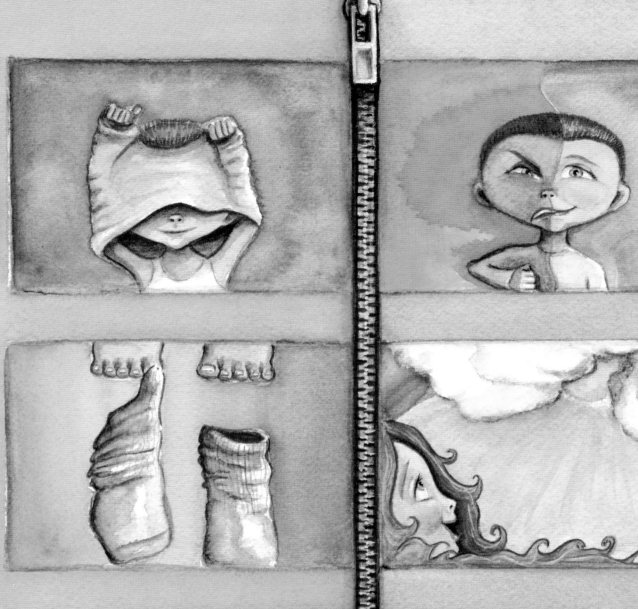

If someone says, "I spilled the beans," she really means that she **told a secret**.

When someone says, "You're the apple of my eye," she really means that **you're terrific**.

If something is a piece of cake, it really means that it is **very easy**.

Home

If someone says, "It's **on the house**," that really means it's **free**.

When someone says, "I **hit the roof**," she really means that she got **very angry**.

If someone says, "That **drives me up a wall**," he really means that **something really annoys him**.

If someone says, "You're the **teacher's pet**," she really means that you're the **teacher's favorite student**.

When someone says, "He's the **class clown**," she really means that he is being **very silly**.

When someone says, "That **rings a bell**," she really means that something **sounds familiar**.

Colors

If someone says, "I passed **with flying colors**," she really means that she did **a great job**.

When someone says, "I have **a green thumb**," she really means that she is **good with plants**.

If someone says, "I'm **tickled pink**," he really means that he is **very happy**.

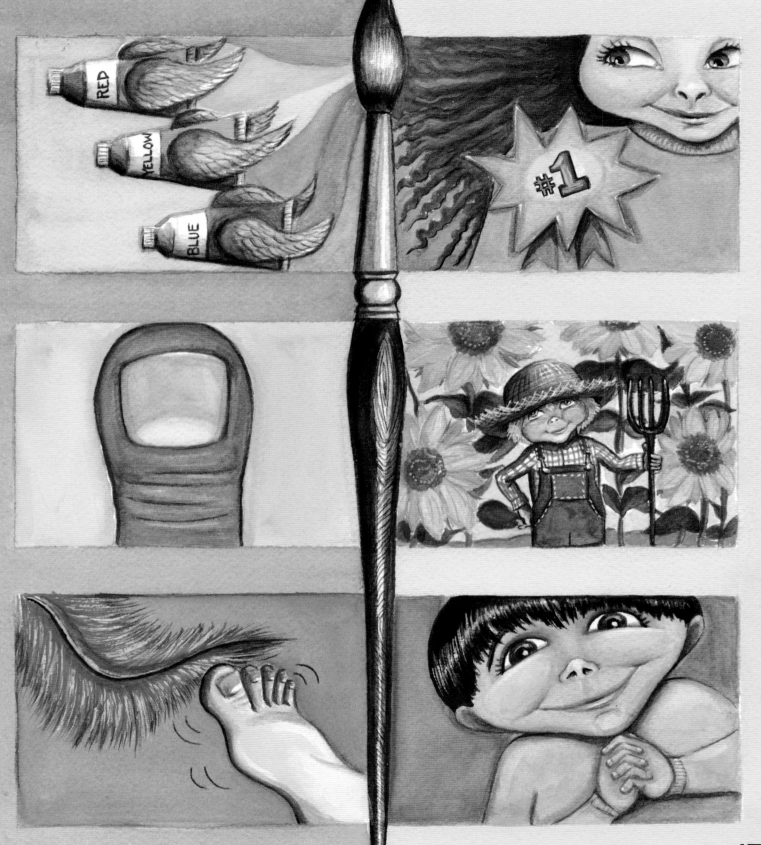

Shapes

When someone says, "I need to go **back to square one**," she really means that she needs to **start over**.

If someone says, "I **ran circles around her**," he really means that he **did a better job**.

If someone says, "I was **bent out of shape**," he really means that he was **irritated**.

Animals

If someone says, "He's into monkey business," she really means that he is being silly.

When someone says, "You need to hold your horses," he really means that you need to be patient.

When someone says, "It's raining cats and dogs," she really means that it's raining very hard.

Insects

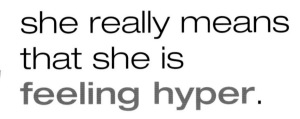

If someone says, "I've got **ants in my pants**," she really means that she is **feeling hyper**.

If someone says, "I have **butterflies in my stomach**," he really means that he is feeling **very nervous**.

When someone says, "She put a **bee in my bonnet**," she really means that someone gave her **something to think about**.

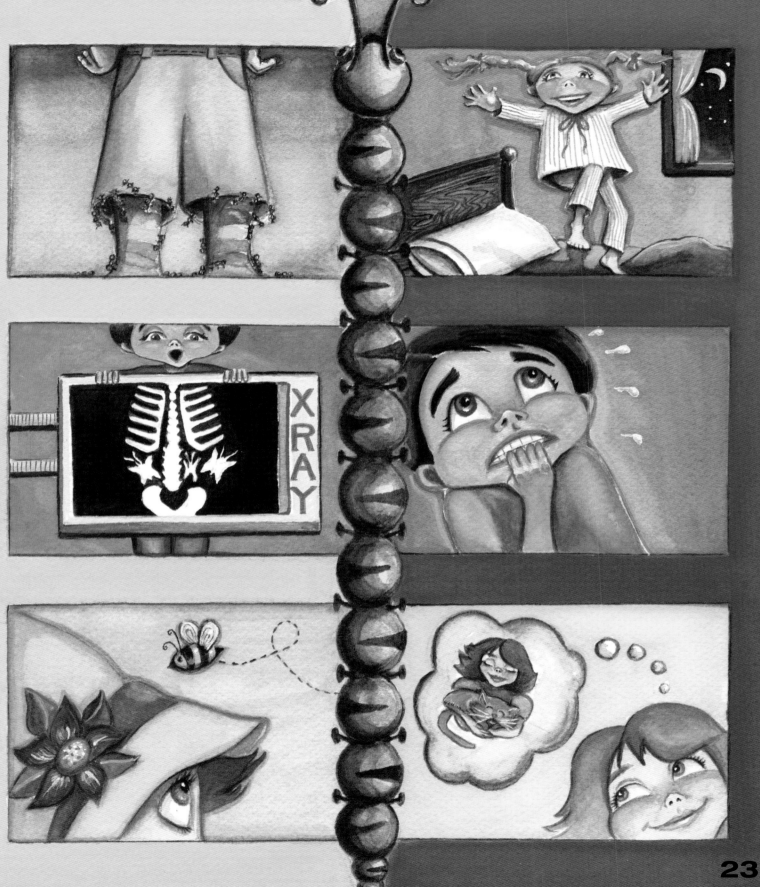

Places

When someone says, "That's **out of this world**," she really means that something is awesome.

If someone says, "I'm **under the weather**,"  she really means that she is feeling sick.

If someone says, "I'm **on cloud nine**," he really means that he is very happy.

Time

When the referee yells, "**Time out**," she really means that it's time to take a break.

If someone says, "I worked **around the clock**," he really means that he worked all day and all night.

If someone says, "My clothes are **second hand**," she really means that her clothes used to belong to someone else.

Numbers

If someone says, "I just **put two and two together**," he really means that he just **figured something out**.

When someone talks about **"the three R's,"** she's really talking about **reading, writing, and arithmetic**.

If someone says, "You're **one in a million**," that really means that you are **very, very special**.

Haverstraw King's Daughters
Public Library

29

Ways to Help Children Internalize the Meanings of the Idioms

The following ideas are intended to turn *Super Silly Sayings That Are Over Your Head* into a super learning tool:

- Give examples of specific situations in which each of the idioms might be used.

- Set up role plays, using exaggerated facial expressions and gestures, to provide the child with a context for learning and an opportunity for practice.

- Model the use of newly learned idioms in natural situations to solidify understanding.

- Set up opportunities for the child to use the newly learned idioms in natural situations to help facilitate generalization.

- Unleash your imagination and let it run wild to provide additional incentives for using the idioms in the real-world environment!